WESTERN BEACONS

WESTERN BEACONS CIRCULAR WALKS

Nick Jenkins

ISBN: 0-86381-638-X

Cover design: Smala, Caernarfon

First published in 2000 by
Gwasg Carreg Gwalch, 12 Iard yr Orsaf, Llanrwst, Wales LL26 0EH
☎ 01492 642031   📠 01492 641502
✆ books@carreg-gwalch.co.uk   Internet: www.carreg-gwalch.co.uk

CONTENTS

About the Author 6

Acknowledgements 7

Introduction 9

Walk 1: The Waterfall Circuit (Pontneddfechan
- Sgwd Clungwyn - Pontneddfechan) 29

Walk 2: From Mellte to Nedd (Ystradfellte
- Blaen Nedd isaf - Porth yr Ogof - Ystradfellte) 33

Walk 3: To the Springs of the Wild Boar (Ystradowen
- Ffrydiau Twrch - Ystradowen) 39

Walk 4: The Lady Beckons (Trecastell Mountain Road
- Llyn y Fan Fach - Trecastell Mountain Road) 43

Walk 5: A Fan - tastic Day Out (Blaen Llia - Fan Gyhirych
- Fan Nedd - Blaen Llia) 47

Walk 6: Where Roman Soldiers Marched (Mynydd Bach
Trecastell - Usk Reservoir - Mynydd Bach Trecastell) 53

Walk 7: Around Loughor's Eye (A Circuit around
Carreg Cennen Castle) 57

Walk 8: Clambering over Cribarth (Craig y Nos
- Cribarth - Craig y Nos) 61

Walk 9: To The Gateway of the Cave (Gwaun Hepste
- Sgwd Clungwyn - Porth yr Ogof - Gwaun Hepste) 67

Walk 10: Over the Fans and Back on the Track
(Blaen Llia - Fan Llia - Fan Frynach - Blaen Llia) 73

Bibliography 76

About The Author

Nick Jenkins is a keen walker and landscape photographer, having walked extensively both at home and abroad. He has produced a number of postcards covering both the Lake District and the Brecon Beacons.

His favourite and most often tramped over areas are the Lake District, North Wales, the Yorkshire Dales, Pembrokeshire and the Brecon Beacons. He has also walked as far afield as the French Alps, Kashmir, Nepal and, more recently, Iceland with his brother-in-law. His first two walking books, *Circular Walks in Gower*, and *Circular Walks in the Black Mountains* are also published by Gwasg Carreg Gwalch.

Nick is also the author of the recently published *Beacons of Light*, the first colour photographic book of the entire Brecon Beacons National Park, and published by D. W. Jones of Port Talbot. In addition, he has contributed a number of walks to walking magazines including 'High' and 'Country Walking'. A number of the walks in this book have previously appeared in 'Country Walking'.

Acknowledgements

The preparation for the walks in this book has eaten into my spare time with a voracious appetite for about a year, and taken me to yet more secret corners of the Park. It has been, once more, a real labour of love even when bending against wind and rain, trying to write up notes in my pocket notebook in conditions in which you wouldn't send a dog out. I have walked and photographed pretty well all of the National Park but, once again, I have discovered hidden recesses of the Park and rediscovered others. Just when you think you know an area well you find you don't! The research, not only for the walks but also for some of the more interesting titbits along the way, has brought me in touch both with places I never knew existed and with stories I have never heard!

The production of the final manuscript has been greatly helped by the assistance and kindness of local people and fellow walkers who have stopped to chat along the way and offer useful snippets of information (little did they realise that, as soon as they were out of sight, I had whipped out my little blue notebook). These, in turn, have been passed on to you. However, I would like to extend particular thanks to the following:

Sue Mabberly (National Park Authority Head Warden); Alan Ward (Central Area Warden), for kindly taking time out to check the legality of rights of way in his area; Frances Morris (again, of the National Park Authority) for all sorts of help and support, and to my wife, Anne, and my son, Stephen, for once more putting up with my many disappearing acts as I put the walks together for this, my third walking book with Gwasg Carreg Gwalch.

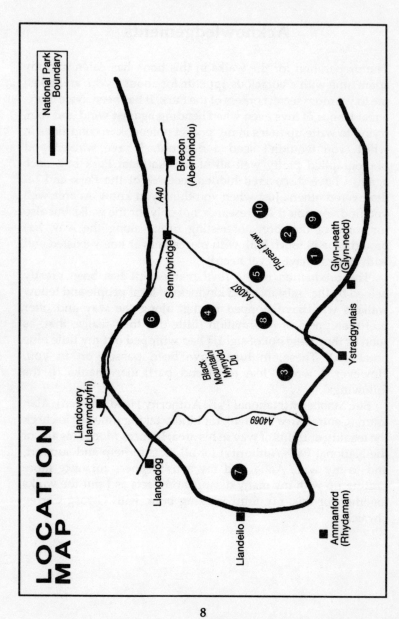

LOCATION MAP

National Park Boundary

Brecon (Aberhonddu)

A40

Sennybridge

Fforest Fawr

Glyn-neath (Glyn-nedd)

A4067

Ystradgynlais

Black Mountain Mynydd Du

A4069

Llandovery (Llanymddyfri)

Llangadog

Llandeilo

Ammanford (Rhydaman)

1 2 3 4 5 6 7 8 9 10

8

Introduction

Desolate, deserted, windswept, wild. All these adjectives sum up the atmosphere of the western section of the Brecon Beacons National Park, referred to for our purposes as the Western Beacons. There are fewer towns and villages and certainly fewer people than in the central and eastern regions of the Park. Not here will you find the acreage of lush, green, cultivated valleys so typical of the Black Mountains; nor here will you find the throngs of multi-coloured walkers (and other assorted tourists), pulled by the magnetic attraction of the heights of Pen y Fan, Corn Du and Cribyn. What you will find, however, are deep wooded valleys, high moorland, whispering grass, sheep by the flock and dramatic windswept scenery. Yes, you will stumble across tourists too, but they tend to congregate around the upper Swansea Valley, focussing on Dan yr Ogof showcaves and Craig y Nos Castle. On a hot summer's day (ha, ha) picnickers also tend to flock to Nant Llia between Fan Llia and Fan Nedd to splash in the river, their cars nose to tail along the roadside. You will find that walkers, too, congregate around the beautiful waterfall area of the upper Neath, or Nedd, valley at Pontneddfechan and Ystradfellte. However, venture into the higher reaches of this unspoiled land and do not be surprised to find yourself utterly alone for quite some time. This, without trying to sound pretentious or elitist, is walking for the connoisseur, for the person who appreciates being alone surrounded by beauty in the form of wilderness. There are sections of the Western Beacons that the National Park Authority will not promote. This may seem a little extreme, but it does echo ecological concerns and serves to emphasise that it is not an area that can sustain mass tourism walking all over it without some damage to the eco-systems. 'Walking with thought' are the keywords here! Or, to misquote from Edward Whymper, the 19th century alpine guide, 'look carefully to every step'.

9

The area I have referred to as the Western Beacons stretches west from the A470 trunk road and encompasses both Fforest Fawr (the Great Forest) and Mynydd Du (the Black Mountain). Don't be misled into thinking there is nothing of interest to the walker in this less populated section of the Park. Nothing could be further from the truth. Here rise the heights of Bannau Sir Gaer (2,460 feet, or 750 metres), Fan Brycheiniog (2,362 feet, or 802 metres) and Fan Gyhirych (2,381 feet or 725 metres). Here, too, plummet the waterfalls of Sgwd yr Eira (the Falls of Snow) and Sgwd Gwladys (attributed to Gwladys, one of the daughters of King Brychan of Brycheiniog), both of which can be walked behind, adding rather a thrill to the proceedings. In between the high contours and deep valleys lie high mountain lakes and reservoirs, few more beautiful or remote than Llyn y Fan Fach and Llyn y Fan Fawr. Your boots will walk you over sandstone, limestone and millstone grit; across grass and heather; along ridges and through wooded gorges. Adding more than a hint of mystery along the way, you will encounter ancient standing stones, stone circles, Iron Age forts and a medieval castle. If that doesn't whet your appetite sell your boots and take up topiary or needlecraft!

Remote the Western Beacons may be but deficient in beauty and adventure they certainly are not. If they lack people it is probably due more to their relative remoteness and lack of publicity than anything else. The whole area is a rich landscape in which the National Park Authority invests considerable time and effort in ensuring it is not trampled to death or spoilt. Only the discerning walker is welcomed here, the walker who appreciates the need to treat the surroundings with the respect they deserve, and who is prepared to invest in a little extra collarwork to reap the rewards that are on offer.

Brief History:

There is relatively scant archaeological evidence of human occupation in the Western Beacons until the Bronze Age, which heralded the arrival of the Beaker Folk from continental Europe. There were certainly Neolithic, or new Stone Age, settlements in the Western Beacons. Indeed, the much told tale of 'The Lady of the Lake' (see 'The Lady Beckons') strongly hints at a settlement on or near Llyn y Fan Fach, but hard evidence is in short supply. The Bronze Age, split into three distinct stages, spanned from approximately around 1,700BC to 700BC, the Beaker Folk earning their name from their intriguing habit of burying pottery beakers in their grave pits.

It seems to be generally agreed that it was the Beaker Folk who were responsible for the standing stone of Maen Llia as well as the stone circle and line arrangements of Cerrig Duon and Saith Maen. Maen Llia (GR 924193) stands all alone just off the top of the mountain road connecting Ystradfellte with Defynnog. The monolith stands 12 feet high by 9 feet across. We will probably never know why it was erected all those years ago, and can only guess that perhaps it served as a route marker or maybe as some sort of monument to ancient spirits. Either way it can still present an eerie sight, standing solitary in its remote location, frequently shrouded in mist or drizzle in the wilderness of Fforest Fawr below Fan Llia.

Cerrig Duon (the Black Stones) is a stone circle or, more precisely, an oval, comprising twenty two small stones, lorded over by one large stone, known as Maen Mawr, or the Great Stone (GR 852207). It is located above the infant Afon Tawe off the mountain road between the upper Swansea Valley (Cwm Tawe) and Trecastle (Trecastell). Rough estimates put the construction of the circle at between 1,700 and 1,200BC, based on the ages of similar circles elsewhere. Again, we can only speculate as to its purpose but in all probability it was some form of temple for worshipping, but whom or what we may never know.

Saith Maen (GR 833153) is about 3 miles (5km) south of Cerrig Duon opposite the northern slopes of Cribarth, and opposite the castle of Craig y Nos. It consists of a row or alignment of seven stones (Saith Maen in Welsh meaning seven stones). It is reckoned that the aligned stones point to Cerrig Duon, but again, the purpose is not clear. The presence of these stones in such remote locations (no minor mountain roads in those days) does, however, add a touch of mystery and intrigue to the Western Beacons.

The Bronze Age was followed by the Iron Age, and spanned the period from around 700BC to 50AD. Here again, the Western Beacons furnish us well with the visible remains of the Iron Age people. Garn Goch (the Red Mound) set above the Tywi valley near Llangadog, (GR 691243) is one of the largest, if not the largest, Iron Age hill-fort in Wales. The site is actually split into two forts, Y Gaer Fach (the Little Fort) and Y Gaer Fawr (the Large Fort). The whole area occupies some 30 acres. Its strategic position is clear and it is quite possible that, when the threat of the Roman invasion of Wales turned into a reality, the Silures (the tribe attributed with the construction of Garn Goch) would have taken refuge behind the huge stone ramparts.

Indeed, it was the Silures, led by their chieftain Caradog (or Caractacus in Hollywood 'speak') who presented the Legions with their first serious opposition as the Roman military machine steadily overran these islands. The extent of the nuisance they presented can be deduced from the size of the Roman marching camps, remains of which are still visible in the Park. These marching camps were, in effect, staging posts connected by the renowned straight 'Roman Roads'. This enabled the Roman army to maintain its grip over its recent and troublesome conquest; a task, incidentally, which was not always successful!

Probably the most visible and impressive of these camps is Y Pigwn to the north of the Usk Reservoir, on the Roman road running along Mynydd-bach Trecastell, connecting the Brecon fort of Y Gaer with the fort at Llandovery. Y Pigwn is estimated to have been capable of accommodating up to 10,000 troops at one time, pretty sizeable even by today's standards. The remnants of a second camp can also be found on the northern slopes of Mynydd y Llan (GR 804263) just off the minor road that runs south of the Usk Reservoir. A third camp, albeit pretty indiscernible on the ground, is passed through in the forestry between Blaen Llia and Maen Madog on the Sarn Helen track.

Although it is quite accurate to say that Rome was the conqueror of this remote tract of upland moor, the empire was never really the owner/occupier of these lands. Judging by the relatively scant archaeological evidence of the Roman occupation, with the exception of the strategic camps and connecting road systems, the garrisons stationed here probably put most of their time, energy and resources into policing their new prize, rather than deriving any major benefits through occupation. Other than the fertile valleys, the rest of the Beacons could offer little in return for the efforts of subjugation and from that point of view the cost of the policing necessary to keep the Silures at arms length probably yielded little, if any, compensation.

Some time after 200AD the Roman army started to pull its troops back towards Rome where much larger problems were starting to loom. This ushered in the period sometimes rather grimly referred to by some as the Dark Ages, or, in complete contrast by others as the Early Christian Period. These were the times of King Brychan, the red haired Irishman who ruled the kingdom of Brycheiniog and, when he had the odd spare moment, fathered thirty-six children. A number of his offspring went on to found religious sites, or cells, many of which are dotted around the Park. The solid power held by King Brychan was maintained, in all probability, as a result of the size of his family. The kingdom of Brycheiniog almost certainly remained intact from around 400AD to the coming of the Normans, and the next 'chapter' in the history of the Park.

The Normans advanced into and across south Wales with a speed of purpose that might well impress military strategists and tacticians of today. Duke William of Normandy and his men invaded in 1066 as every schoolboy knows, landing in Pevensey Bay and, by 1067, were starting to put up defensive motte and bailey fortifications on the eastern edge of the Park (the Normans paid scant regard to Park Authority planning regulations, it would appear!). Most of the fortresses along the Welsh/English border had been established by William Fitzosbern, the Earl of Hereford. Unfortunately, for Fitzosbern, he and King William fell out and William turned to his half brother, Bernard de Neufmarche, to protect the borderlands. By 1088, de Neufmarche (sometimes anglicised to Newmarch, although he came from Neufmarche in Normandy) had started to make incursions into Wales. By 1091 his army had occupied Brecon and by 1110 he more or less imposed his rule on the region previously covered by Brycheiniog, and had established himself as the first Marcher Lord of Brecon. Marcher Lords were afforded considerable leeway in the way they ran the Marches, possibly a tactic employed by the king to ensure little trouble from the occupants to the west of Offa's Dyke. The significance of de Neufmarche in the Western Beacons is in his establishment of the hunting area we know today as Fforest Fawr, the Great Forest. The word 'forest' did not, and does not, necessarily imply huge tracts of trees. Rather, it defines an expanse of land, a 'royal preserve for hunting', although the tag 'royal' came along a little later, as we shall see. The Forest was governed by its own sets of rules. Rules, it must be said, that were harsh in the extreme if anyone should be unfortunate enough to be caught flaunting them. De Neufmarche would have added land to the Forest as he saw fit, the occupants having little say in the matter.

Fforest Fawr would have been the playground of the Lord of Brecon as well as his friends and guests. Should any unauthorised persons dare to enter the Forest or, worse, be discovered with any evidence that they had been hunting, their fate could be a public maiming or even execution. Such foolish forays would be reported by the retainers employed to maintain the Forest for the Lord, including the constable, (the chief forester in effect) and the watchers or 'regarders'.

The area covered by Fforest Fawr in medieval times was considerable, stretching approximately from Afon Twrch and the Fan Hir ridge in the west to Afon Tarell in the east and from the River Usk (Afon Wysg) in the north to just above Penderyn in the south. The tops of Fan Gyrych, Fan Nedd, Fan Llia and Fan Fawr all fell within its boundaries. There was, incidentally, also a Fforest Fach (or Fechan) which covered a much smaller area between Sennybridge and Crai (Cray).

Fforest Fawr, like any hunting park, would have been a working forest with farms, mills, manor houses and grazing land all within its boundaries. The tag 'royal' came about following the execution of Henry Stafford, Lord of Brecon and Duke of Buckingham, when the Forest was seized by the crown in 1483, thus being accorded true royal status. Stafford, along with Bishop Morton of Ely, stood accused of plotting to overthrow King Richard III. During the reign of King Richard the harsh Forest laws were relaxed a little, with charges for grazing being reduced and punishment for infringement of the laws being lessened to fines; infinitely better than mutilation or death! In fact it was from this point on that the history of Fforest Fawr stabilised right up to the Enclosure Acts of 1815 and 1819. The fast flowing rivers, Afon Pyrddin, Afon Nedd, Afon Tringarth, and Afon Llia (the latter two subsequently meeting to become the Afon Mellte, provided ample power to drive mill wheels for grinding corn, of which there were seven recorded in the area. The occupants of the Forest were very much occupants rather than owners, beholden in one way or another to the Lord of the Manor.

Then, in 1815, the first of the two Enclosure Acts more or less put an end to this feudal life once and for all. The lower reaches and peripheries of the Forest were sold off to the highest bidders, the remainder being split between the commoners and the crown. At the same time the payment of all forest dues was

15

abolished. It was around this time that sheep farming started to expand rapidly, vast tracts of the upland moors being given over to grazing. The Cnewr Company bought a considerable acreage around the middle of the 19th century, centring on Fan Gyhirych and Fan Nedd, and today is one of the largest landowners in the area. The Cnewr Estate is the only large upland area in the Park where access to the public is not freely available.

The Landscape:

In common with the rest of the National Park, the vast majority of the Western Beacons lies on a bed of Devonian, or Old Red Sandstone. The top north-west corner, from the Usk reservoir to Llanymddyfri (Llandovery) lies on the sedimentary rocks known as Silurian (named by some discerning geologist after the Brythonic Silures tribe). Moving south we cross over the red sandstone belt roughly as far as Ystradfellte at which point we find ourselves in limestone country. Continuing south we meet millstone grit followed finally by the stuff on which south Wales was built, king coal.

All of this is a bit of an over simplification of something rather more complex than can be explained away in four sentences, so, herewith follows a slightly more comprehensive foray into the geology of the Western Beacons!

Old Red Sandstone, laid down some 370 million years ago, (sometimes referred to as Devonian, and understood by those familiar with the rock colouring along the south Devon coastline) is the prevailing rock type, accounting for about 70% of the bedrock of the National Park. It owes its red tint to the quantity of iron found in the rock. A notable feature of old red sandstone is the way it weathers, leaving huge, sweeping escarpments following from west to east across the northern edge of the Park. This is seen to dramatic effect from the summit of Tyle Gwyn, above and to the west of Llyn y Fan Fach, as the cliffs of Bannau Sir Gaer rise one after the other into the

16

distance. Visible from here, too, are the layers of Brownstones, a sub-division of Old Red Sandstone. Another key feature of this rock type is the way water carves out deep 'V' shaped grooves and gullies as it alternately trickles and tumbles down the cliff face to the lower scree slopes or, as at Bannau Sir Gaer, into Llyn y Fan Fach.

Moving further south we start to encounter carboniferous limestone. This belt extends for some 6 to 7 miles (9.5 to 11 kilometres) after the sandstone, altering the hitherto smoothed and rounded southern slopes of the Black Mountains to resemble more closely a lunar landscape. Here are sinkholes, or swallets, as they are sometimes known, big enough to lose a man in, piles of limestone boulders and a much more shattered surface altogether. One place to see this at its best is in the Ogof Ffynnon Ddu National Nature Reserve, encountered in the walk over Fan Gyhirych. Originally laid down in shallow seas during the Silurian period, some 300 to 400 million years ago, the limestone is full of the fossilised remains of sea flora and fauna. Around Afon Nedd and Afon Pyrddin are to be found a few fairly small examples of limestone pavements, together with the characteristic clints and grykes so often associated with the larger pavements found in the Yorkshire Dales. In some areas, but still within this narrow band of limestone, a belt of basal, or millstone grit, overlies it. This hard rock is made up of quartzite and sandstones and earns its name from the fact that it was once used as the material for millstones. The rivers that start to build some momentum in the south-western area of the Park flow across the hard gritstone to plummet over fault lines between the grit and the limestone. A superb example of this can be seen at Pont Cwm Pwll-y-rhyd, where Afon Nedd disappears between limestone and millstone grit, to re-appear some 1km downstream (GR 902140). In between are a dry riverbed and gorge, known locally as the Grand Canyon. Where these cracks, or faults, are underlaid with softer shales, or even thin seams of coal, the pressure of the falling water has cut back a space behind some of the falls to the extent that it is perfectly possible to walk behind them. Two excellent examples of such undercutting can be seen at Sgwd yr Eira on Afon Hepste and Sgwd Gwladys on Afon Pyrddin.

In these limestone areas are some of the most dramatic cave systems to be found in Wales, and possibly Britain. Limestone is highly soluble in rainwater and presents a ready target for the onslaught of both rainwater and river water. The water when added to limestone, forms carbonic acid and this, combined with the acid contained in the drain water which has passed through peat higher up in the hills, has the effect of eating away at the limestone along weaknesses, forming tunnels. Certainly the best known caves are the Dan yr Ogof showcaves in the Tawe valley above Craig y Nos, but many other caves and tunnels are known to speliologists from all over the country. Porth yr Ogof, on Afon Mellte below Ystradfellte, is an enormous cavern retreating some 200 feet (60m) in total, and from which a number of tunnels continue underground. It is possible to follow part of the complex to re-emerge downstream where the river resurfaces. Probably the most significant complex, however, is that of Ogof Ffynnon Ddu. This was at one time and may still be, the longest and deepest cave system in Britain. The Ogof Ffynnon Ddu complex is closed to the public due to its technical difficulties and the potential danger but it is a component part of the Ogof Ffynnon Ddu National Nature Reserve, being of considerable international geological importance. The caves of Porth yr Ogof, whilst not in the same league as Ogof Ffynnon Ddu, should still not be attempted unless with competent and qualified guides. It is perfectly possible to enter the main chamber, known as the White Horse cave because of streaks of calcite in the chamber in the shape of a horse's head, but if uninitiated in the skills of the mole, you are best advised to confine exploration to this area alone, and not to go wriggling off down one of the numerous side passages. The 'doom and gloom' notices around the area warn of fatalities that have occurred here – they are not a bluff. Flash floods do occur and fill the passages very quickly indeed. Even experienced cavers have been known to become seriously unstuck here. Another cave can be found at the source of Afon Llwchwr, across the valley from the limestone fortress of Carreg Cennen.

Our next rock layer is another form of carboniferous rock but this time with a much closer association with south Wales – coal. Coal is the product of decaying forest vegetation which turned to peat which, in turn, was buried by muds and sands brought down by rivers. The weight of these muds and sands slowly compacted and crushed the peat to form coal. The coal beds only comprise a comparatively small sliver of the south-western corner, predominantly around the area of Ystradgynlais, and north of Upper and Lower Cwmtwrch and Ystradowen. Within the Park boundary, near Ystradowen, lies the ruin of Brynhenllys colliery, opened in 1872 and closed down in 1955.

The Walks:

As mentioned earlier, the relatively gentle and rolling nature of the terrain prevents walks in the Western Beacons from ever really being too severe. Nowhere is the walking particularly difficult (unless you've allowed the good life to get the better of you). There are few crags or other rocky excrescences to get caffled up in; in fact the only real opportunities to get hand to rock are up on Cribarth and, to a lesser extent, on some of the limestone outcrops in the remote moorland just to the east of Sinc y Giedd. The greatest challenges to your legs will certainly be on the routes up onto Fan Gyhirych, Fan Hir, Fan Brycheiniog and Bannau Sir Gaer, but it has to be said that even these ascents are not particularly arduous (with the possible exception of the ascent up onto Fan Gyhirych from the A4067 road). It is the wilderness walking in these parts that really gives the Western Beacons their reputation as 'leg stretching' country.

All the walks described in this book fall within the area to the west of the Taf and Tarell valleys, defined by the main A470 trunk road. One walk sits ever so slightly outside the National Park boundary, and that is the approach, along Afon Nedd to its confluence with Afon Pyrddin. This area is managed by the Neath Port Talbot County Borough Council but the Park Authority and the Council work closely together in this area.

As I noted in *Circular Walks in the Black Mountains* any criteria laid down for grading a walk are bound to be subjective. What for one walker is a pleasant stroll could be of Himalayan proportions to another. All sorts of variables creep in to thwart the formulas; I would be hard pressed to walk according to the well publicised Naismith's Formula which fails utterly to allow for stops to capture the scenery (or several deep breaths after a grinding uphill climb), to take photographs or to grab a lunch break. For this reason I have graded the walks in this area more in terms of their length rather than in terms of their ascent and descent. By this criterion a long, but relatively ascent and descent free walk could end up being graded as strenuous. Entirely arbitrarily, therefore, I have laid down the following guidelines. They are meant to be just that, and hopefully should help you plan when deciding if you are tackling a day walk or an afternoon stroll. As a loose rule of thumb I normally allow for an average of about 2 miles an hour; that seems to cover ups, downs and a few stops.

- relatively few inclines   Easy
- some uphill collarwork   Moderate
- fairly long walk, possibly involving
  some ascents/descents   Strenuous

The introduction to each walk indicates the nature of the terrain that you will encounter, and I have not allowed myself to become too hidebound by the above criteria if it doesn't seem sensible to do so.

All distances are quoted in good old imperial measurements but have their metric equivalent bracketed after them. Neither measurement should be construed as being absolutely definitive. Where distances have not been quoted, it is intended that the landmarks indicated in the text are so obvious as to render the quoting of yardage a bit irrelevant.

In terms of how to kit up for walking in the Western Beacons it is vital to bear a few pointers in mind. A significant amount of the walking described is relatively remote and on exposed hillsides and moorland, offering precious little in the way of shelter. The highest point reached is 'only' 2,632 feet (802 metres), on Fan Brycheiniog, but it can be mightily unpleasant when a fog comes down or rain whips your face. Weather can be very fickle on high ground and the nature of the terrain hereabouts gives little away in the form of shelter or landmarks. In short, be properly prepared. Bring spare clothing (particularly pullovers or fleeces and socks), a map, compass, torch and whistle. Also kit up with food and drink – nothing beats a flask of piping hot tomato soup delicately sipped on a mountain top. Know that, if the worst comes to the worst, the emergency distress signal is 6 blasts on a whistle or flashes on a torch (or loud shouts if necessary), followed by a minute's pause, then repeated. The acknowledgement is three blasts/flashes/shouts.

The nature of the land is also such that there are tracts of black, soft and gooey muck on the upper reaches (referred to as peat, by those who know about such things), and no shortage of mud lower down in the valleys, so wrap your feet and legs up in something supportive and as waterproof as possible. Gaiters are preferable to carrier bags (that said I've seen people line their boots very successfully with carrier bags).

In terms of what to carry your gear in, a rucksack of between 20 and 45 litres capacity should be plenty for all your accoutrements and sustenance. In fact a 45 litre sack would probably be enough for two (unless you are planning an 'eatathon'). For the walks in this book anything over 45 litres capacity, although impressive to lesser mortals, could become burdensome (any such wearer is probably setting off on, or coming to the end of the walk that traverses the Park, or is a soldier out on manoeuvres – don't even ask to feel the weight of their sacks).

Another fairly recent development in hill-walking is the use of walking, or trekking poles. Initially I was somewhat sceptical regarding the benefits claimed from their use but now am a confirmed convert. There is little doubt that they relieve pressure on the knees when descending, and I find going uphill a whole lot easier too!

The following maps cover all the walks in this guide:
- Ordnance Survey Landranger 160 – Brecon Beacons (Bannau Brycheiniog)
- Ordnance Survey Outdoor Leisure 12 – Western Area, Llandeilo and the Black Mountain
- Ordnance Survey Outdoor Leisure 11 – Central Area, Brecon and the Beacons
- Harveys The Walker's Map – Brecon Beacons (Bannau Brycheiniog)
- Harveys Superwalker – Brecon Beacons West

The purchase of one, or all of, the above maps is strongly recommended in order to get the most out of the excellent walking to be had in this region. Apart from providing definitive routes and rights of way, the maps can help you work out some extensions, short cuts or deviations to the walks described in the book. This could be especially helpful if you decide to opt for the Beacons Bus service, in terms of selecting appropriate drop off and pick up points (contact the National Park Authority in Brecon for details). Where I have specified the relevant maps in the introduction to each walk, note that I have only referenced the 1:25,000 maps.

A sketch map accompanies each walk in the book. I should point out, however, that I am no cartographer and my sad but amusing little sketch maps can only really act as an approximate

22

guide; they must be treated as such, the map being your definitive route bible. The sketch maps do, however, make a valiant attempt to show the points of interest detailed after each walk, the number of each point corresponding with the text. One general point I was taught regarding navigation and map reading is to always check the map as you progress, and be as aware as you can of your whereabouts at all times. To try and orientate yourself when lost, especially if the weather closes in, can prove to be mightily difficult. Always seek to establish where you are going, rather than try and confirm where you have been!

It is also important to note that whilst every effort has been made to ensure that the details contained in the walks are as up to date as possible, nothing stands still, not least the countryside. From time to time, gates appear or disappear; stiles are renewed or upgraded; paths are renewed, extended, diverted or even closed altogether. This happens from time to time in the Park, as the authority negotiates or re-negotiates rights of way with local landowners. Once or twice whilst compiling this guide I have had to revise walk details where a gate suddenly decided to become a stile, or a path had been diverted (e.g. the ascent of Cribarth has recently been re-routed). Indeed, on one of the walks (the walk up to the summit of Fan Llia), what was once a concrete bridge is now a ford! Hopefully, such changes in detail should be fairly minor and not detract from the enjoyment of the walk. Any difficult or dangerous obstructions, however, should always be reported to the Rights of Way team at the Brecon Beacons National Park Authority, who act as custodians of public rights of way on behalf of the local authorities.

The 'Rights of Way' team is based at the Park Authority's Headquarters in Brecon. In brief the work of the team involves the following:-

Maintaining and keeping under review the definitive map – this is the legal document relating to rights of way.

The team has a duty to sign all rights of way where they meet a metalled road and has the power to install signs and directional waymarks to assist landowners with rights of way on their property and to ensure people using them are on the correct line. This is clearly in evidence in most of our walks; yellow arrows indicating footpaths which are a right of way, white arrows indicating permitted paths and blue indicating bridleways: look out for them.

Network maintenance – the team is active in maintaining and, where possible, improving rights of way within the Authority's area.

Legal matters – the Authority has legal powers to enforce and protect the public's right to use and enjoy rights of way and also to undertake diversions and modification orders where deemed necessary by law.

There are many kilometres of permitted footpaths and rights of way within the Western Beacons. The 'Rights of Way' team relies heavily on reports from walkers, riders and other users on conditions, obstructions or general problems encountered. Should you have anything to report, as mentioned earlier, or want further information about these routes or the wider network then please contact the Wardens' Head Office at Glamorgan Street, Brecon, telephone number (01874) 624437. Reassuringly, many local people I meet whilst researching the walks are most welcoming of those who chose to come and explore their homeland on foot and, provided proper care is taken, problems are seldom encountered.

One last point well worth bearing in mind is the weather – the Park has plenty of it! In hilly regions weather patterns can vary from valley to valley and altitude always results in drops in temperature. It is always a good idea to find out what can be expected, so that the walk can be planned accordingly. In any event, be aware that the weather here can change suddenly and without warning.

Welsh Place Names:

Non-Welsh speakers (which, for the record, includes me), miss-out on a wealth of beauty and history by not being able to speak and read it, but to understand a few words, especially in the context of place names on the map, can add significantly to your enjoyment of a walk, if not for your partner as you spit and growl your feeble efforts at them! I have attempted here a list of some of the more common names encountered in the Western Beacons; it is not exhaustive! After that you're on your own.

Pen – head or top
Rhos – moorland
Llan – church, or holy place
Cefn – ridge
Bryn – hill
Cwm – valley
Du – black
Cil – narrow
Mynydd – hill or mountain
Hen – old
Llys – court
Maen – rock or stone
Pwll – pool
Du – black
Gwern – marshland
Ffrwd – stream
Waun – pasture or moorland
Nant – valley or stream
Crug – hillock

Mawr(Fawr) – great
Ffordd – way or road
Sarn – way or road
Tal – end
Garth – hill or enclosure
Fach(fechan) – little
Allt – height, or slope/hill
Capel – chapel
Ffin – border or boundary
Pont – bridge
Fan/Bannau – peak/s
Sarn – way
Hir – long
Sgwd – waterfall
Llyn – lake
Blaen – end
Carreg/Cerrig – rock/s
melin – mill

Do not make the mistake of trying to locate the village of Llwybr Cyhoeddus, liberally signposted but never found. It is Welsh for public footpath (just look on the other side of the sign if you do not believe me). Remember also that 'f' is pronounced 'v' in Welsh.

Conservation:

One last but vitally important point does need stressing before we set off on our walks. The National Park is an exceptionally beautiful area under increasing pressure to provide leisure and amenities to an ever growing tourist influx. The recent improvements in the road network, especially recent additions and improvements to the M4 motorway and the main A470 trunk road make the Park so much more accessible to far more people than ever before. There are certain things that we walkers, as a constituent part of this tourist demand, can do to help preserve the beauty of the Park for both our own and our children's enjoyment. Always walk with care and consideration; marching up a hill, ten abreast will do wonders for erosion and the resulting scars will take much longer to heal than they do to create! Be aware of, and considerate towards, your surroundings. For example, don't ever scramble over walls or leave gates open (unless they were open when you found them). They are there for a reason and if breached or left open can cause untold misery to farmers controlling their stock, especially at breeding time. I know this is a mantra fixed in the minds of responsible walkers but there are many who still forget or simply don't realise the consequences of their actions. Similarly, don't jettison your rubbish *en route*. There are few sights more ugly, environmentally damaging and completely avoidable than empty drinks cans, bottles and crisp packets just discarded along the paths. They were in your rucksack when full so they can't be that much of a burden to carry back when they're empty! Apart from anything else, they present a real danger to livestock that could so easily choke on thoughtlessly thrown away junk. Be aware that the National Park Authority currently has a policy of not promoting the area around Llyn y Fan Fach and Llyn y Fan Fawr. This is directly an attempt to minimise damage to, or misuse of, an ecologically sensitive area. No-one can stop us walking there and the Park Authority recognises that – it is just an indication of their concern for the minimising of path erosion and other damage that inconsiderate people can wreak. Remember, above all, that the Western Beacons (and, indeed, the rest of the National Park) are there to be enjoyed – but not just by you.

The Country Code:

- enjoy the countryside and respect its life and work
- guard against all risk of fire
- keep your dog under close control – especially important in this area!
- keep to public paths across farmland
- use gates and stiles to cross fences, hedges and walls
- leave livestock, crops and machinery alone
- take your litter home
- help to keep all water clean
- protect wildlife, plants and trees
- take special care on country roads
- don't make any unnecessary noise
- As the old adage eloquently puts it, 'leave nothing but footprints, take nothing but memories' (or photographs, depending on where you may have previously read it!).

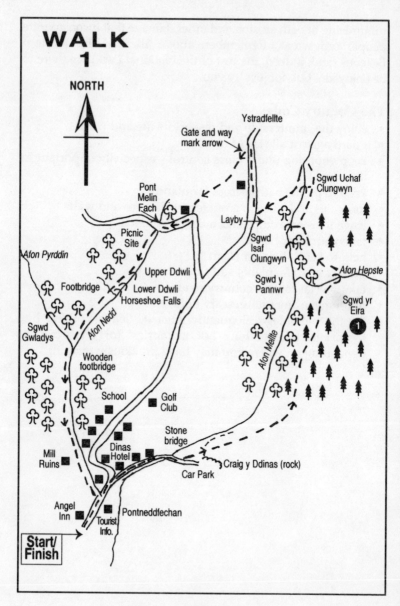

WALK 1

NORTH

Ystradfellte

Gate and way mark arrow

Sgwd Uchaf Clungwyn

Pont Melin Fach

Layby

Afon Pyrddin

Picnic Site

Sgwd Isaf Clungwyn

Afon Hepste

Upper Ddwli

Sgwd y Pannwr

Footbridge

Lower Ddwli
Horseshoe Falls

Afon Nedd

Sgwd yr Eira

Sgwd Gwladys

Afon Mellte

Wooden footbridge

School

Golf Club

Stone bridge

Mill Ruins

Dinas Hotel

Craig y Ddinas (rock)

Car Park

Angel Inn

Pontneddfechan

Tourist Info.

Start/Finish

28

The Waterfall Circuit
(Pontneddfechan - Sgwd Clungwyn
- Pontneddfechan)

Maps:	O S Outdoor Leisure 11 – Central Area, Brecon and the Beacons Harveys Superwalker – Brecon Beacons West
Access:	The walk starts and ends at the Angel Inn, Pontneddfechan
Start/Parking:	Car Park at GR 900077.
Distance/Grade:	About 8 miles (12.9 kilometres). Strenuous, on account of the length involved and the roughness of some of the terrain around Afon Nedd.
Terrain:	Mostly good tracks and paths, but with some road walking. Expect mud after periods of rain, rendering some stretches slippery. Take care and no problems should arise.
Facilities:	Pub and loos at the start/end. Try the White Horse in the High Street; excellent welcome and home cooked food. Tourist Information Centre also at the start with useful information on the area (worth a visit). There is also a small shop stocking food and drink on the Pontneddfechan to Ystradfellte road (passed *en route*).
Note:	The waterfalls are seen at their best after a good downpour, which is when the paths and rocks around here are at their most slippery. Do take care and keep young offspring on a fairly tight rein.

The Walk:

With your back to the Angel Inn, turn left along the road and continue ahead to pass the Dinas Hotel on your right. Don't turn left up the hill but follow the road ahead, passing a row of houses on your left, to cross a stone bridge over the Afon Mellte. Turn left onto a path on the right bank of the river looking for a footpath sign to Sgwd yr Eira (keep the large, and now fenced off, Dinas Rock to your right). Stay with the path for about 1¹/₂ miles (2.4 kilometres) as it crosses the moorland slopes of Moel Penderyn before descending through woodland to Sgwd yr Eira. These are our first, and most impressive, falls on Afon Hepste. Take care on the descent, the path can be slippery here.

Continue along the path as it proceeds behind the falling curtain of water along a rocky ledge (quite exciting, this bit). On reaching the far bank turn left and follow the obvious path up the steps on your right. On reaching the top of the steps turn left and follow the path to Afon Mellte. Paths have recently been redirected hereabouts so it is now necessary to descend to see the next two falls on our circuit; Sgwd y Pannwr (the Fuller's Falls, named after the 'sudsy' effect obtained after washing fleeces in water with fuller's earth) and Sgwd Isaf Clungwyn. This is done by taking a path to the left by a large solitary tree and descending fairly steeply. Sgwd y Pannwr is on the left at the bottom, with Sgwd Isaf Clungwyn a little up river. Retrace your steps back up the hill to regain the path left earlier. Turn left and follow the path as it winds its way alongside forestry to emerge above the falls of Sgwd Uchaf Clungwyn. Follow the path slightly further uphill then round to the left and downhill to a wooden bridge. Cross the bridge, turn half left to ascend through the woods and continue along the track, passing Clungwyn Farm, to emerge on the road that joins Pontneddfechan (to the left) with Ystradfellte (to the right).

Turn right, and continue along the road for about 500 yards (460 meters) passing both a shop and petrol station on your left and a chapel on your right. Where the road bends sharp right take a farm track on the left and through a gate. Look out for a National Park sign on the left-hand gatepost. Follow the track, passing the farms of Heol Fawr and Glyn Mercher Uchaf to a lane. At the lane turn right to descend to Pont Melin Fach (the remains of the mill being just visible upstream from the bridge on the east bank) and a picnic site.

Cross the bridge, turn left through the picnic site to its far end and cross a stile into woods, Afon Nedd (sometimes referred to as the Nedd Fechan) on your left. Keep to the path, following the river down stream, taking care in one or two places. Pass first the Upper Ddwli Falls then the Lower Ddwli Falls. The path descends to a wooden bridge, on the left of which are the Horseshoe Falls. In spring, the puddles that gather in the limestone pavement between the Horseshoe and Lower Ddwli Falls are a Mecca for spawning toads. After appropriate exploration, cross the bridge that spans the narrow Nant Llechau, and continue along the path. One or two stretches are prone to deep mud along here, as is the end of this stretch of the path where Afon Nedd and Afon Pyrddin meet (not so much mud as a veritable bog at times). At the confluence of the rivers you have a choice: either turn right and follow the east bank of the Afon Pyrddin to Sgwd Gwladys or cross the new wooden bridge (erected June 1999) and turn right to view it from the west bank (or do both – it's worth it!). It is possible to follow the east bank of the Pyrddin past Sgwd Gwladys to the remote falls of Sgwd Einion Gam (the Falls of the Crooked Anvil), but you really are in uncharted land here. The path 'isn't', and several crossings of the river will be needed. There are those who say these are the most dramatic of the falls but I haven't got there yet – so do let me know!

From Sgwd Gwladys retrace your steps (and cross the bridge to the west bank if necessary) and continue along the clear path down the course of the Nedd. After about a mile (1.6 kilometres) you will emerge back behind the Angel Inn and the start of the walk.

Points of Interest:

Sgwd yr Eira, the 'Waterfall of Snow', is probably the best known waterfall in the area. It has also been known as the Upper Cilhepste Fall, as distinct from the Lower Cilhepste Fall, further downstream. The falls offer a slice of adventure in having a path (indeed, our route!) run behind the curtain of water, attributable to the cutting away of the soft shales by the persistent backsplash from the tumbling water. Indeed this feature was the subject of a fine painting 'Shepherds Passing Behind Cilhepste Fall', to be found in the National Museum of Wales. After rain the falls are stupendous, if a little deafening, a foaming sheet of water crashing some 50 to 60 feet (15 to 18 meters) over a ledge to the deep plunge pool below. Enjoy, but do take care; the rocks hereabouts can be very slippery.

From Mellte to Nedd

(Ystradfellte - Blaen Nedd Isaf - Porth yr Ogof - Ystradfellte)

Maps:	O S Outdoor Leisure 11 – Central Area, Brecon and the Beacons
	Harveys Superwalker – Brecon Beacons West
Access:	The walk starts and ends in the village of Ystradfellte, disconcertingly close to the New Inn.
Start/Parking:	Ystradfellte village car park (free!) GR 929134
Distance/Grade:	About 7 miles (11.3 kilometres). Strenuous, more on account of the nature of some of the terrain encountered than the length involved.
Terrain:	Mostly good forestry and grass tracks and paths, but with some stretches of indistinct path.
Facilities:	The New Inn is right next door to the car park, and there are loos in the village, opposite the church (albeit that the Gents has no roof). There are also loos in the car park at Porth yr Ogof.
Note:	Parts of this walk, along Sarn Helen, can be very wet, especially after heavy rain. Wear something waterproof from the kneecaps down (boots and gaiters would seem a good idea).

The Walk:

Leave the back of the car park by way of a path onto the lane. Turn left up the lane and pass through a gate. The lane soon

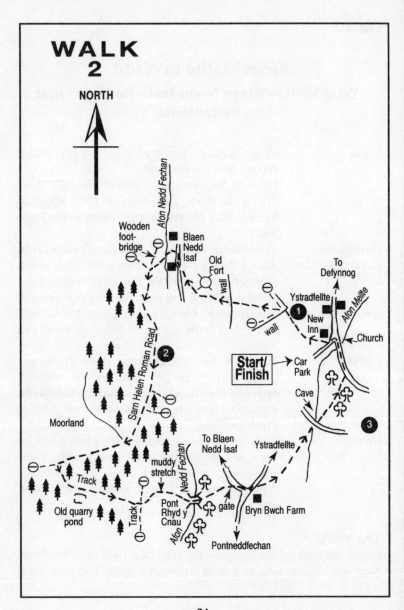

WALK 2

NORTH

Afon Nedd Fechan

Wooden foot-bridge

Blaen Nedd Isaf

Old Fort

wall

wall

To Defynnog

Ystradfellte ❶

New Inn

Church

Afon Mellte

Sarn Helen Roman Road

❷

Start/Finish

Car Park

Cave

❸

Moorland

muddy stretch

To Blaen Nedd Isaf

Ystradfellte

Track

Nedd Fechan

Track

Old quarry pond

Pont Rhyd y Cnau

gate

Bryn Bwch Farm

Afon

Pontneddfechan

comes to an end at a sign indicating Tyle Farm to the right. Continue ahead, however, up a stony track. Follow the track to the point where it enters open moorland through a gate in a wall.

Take care here to follow the direction of the wooden post indicating the bridleway to Blaen Nedd Isaf. Do not follow either the path left to Dyffryn Nedd or the obvious track straight ahead. The bridleway is clear on the map but not clear on the ground. For confidence, take a bearing west on 300 degrees and cross rough moor, looking carefully for a gate and stile near the top of the hill ahead (note that the OS map marks a fort on top of the hill you are making for). Gently descend to cross a track and ascend the hill where the path becomes a little more obvious. Pass through the gate (or cross the stile) onto a clearer track, round the base of the hill then turn left onto a path. Do not follow the track that continues north beneath the base of the hill. Follow the path (marked with the occasional bridleway arrow) to crest a gentle ridge and descend through rough pasture, then a field to cross a stile into a lane.

Turn right into the lane and continue ahead to the farm of Blaen Nedd Isaf. The farm dogs here may greet you; they are noisy but harmless. Pass in front of the house and turn left through a gate, with the farm buildings on your right. Swing right to pass more farm buildings and descend to a footbridge. Pass through a small gate onto the bridge to cross Afon Nedd Fechan. Continue ahead uphill, a metal gate on your left, to pass through a wooden gate into a field. Keep to the left edge of the field to leave it over another stile. You are now on the Roman road of Sarn Helen.

Turn left to pass, almost immediately, through a gate. Bear left, as clearly indicated on a nearby signpost, to continue along Sarn Helen. The Roman road will now be your guide for almost two miles (3.2 kilometres). After about a mile (1.6 kilometres), and where forest is met on the left you will pass first one, then a second, post indicating footpaths off to the left to Dyffryn

Nedd. Ignore them both and continue along Sarn Helen. At this point you will notice forest on both sides of the track. Note the point where the forest terminates on your right, to become open moorland. About 1/2 mile (800 metres) later look for a metal gate and a stile on your left onto a track leading into the forest. In fact they indicate the next path after the second path to Dyffryn Nedd passed earlier (again, as a guide, if you pass a substantial upright stone in the forest fence boundary on your left you have gone too far). Pass through this gate onto the track and follow it for about 1/2 mile (800 metres) to the point where it meets another broad track at right angles. Turn left and, about 10 yards/metres later turn 1/2 right onto an earth track. Follow the earth (sand and mud in places) track as it descends through the forest to the bridge at Pont Rhyd-y-cnau, (the 'bridge at the ford of the nuts'; is a not an unreasonable name, given the quantity of hazel trees hereabouts).

Cross the bridge over Afon Nedd Fechan and ascend the steep and stony track opposite, signposted to Gwaun Bryn Bwch. The track has become quite badly eroded and, whilst presenting no serious problems, should nevertheless be tackled with care. (A local did tell me that, some years ago, someone tried – and failed – to drive a truck down here!). The track ends at a gate on the lane leading to Blaen Nedd Isaf. Pass through the gate and turn right into the lane. Continue, to meet the road from Pontneddfechan to Ystradfellte. Turn left at this junction and, about 20 yards (18 metres) later, turn 1/2 right through a gate into a field, following the waymarked track to Porth yr Ogof. The track, now gravelled, leaves the field by way of a leafy lane. Where the lane opens up, about 20 yards (18 metres) later, turn left to cross a waymarked stile and gate into a green lane. Follow the green lane unerringly for about 1/2 mile (800m), passing through several wooden gates, to finally emerge at a tarmac lane by the car park at Porth yr Ogof.

From here, the path to Porth yr Ogof is clearly waymarked should you wish to visit it. To continue on the walk, however, make for the end of the car park, to leave it over a waymarked stile. Follow the waymarked footpath as it leads along field edges and copses, to join a lane leading to Ystradfellte. The path joins the lane at a stile above Porth yr Ogof Farm. Turn left down the lane to return to the village, the car park and (if open) the pub, for a well-deserved refresher (when crossing the bridge over Afon Mellte just before entering the village take a careful look up and down the river for herons fishing).

Points of Interest:

Ystradfellte is a small hill-farming hamlet high in the Mellte valley. The village, minimalist in its contents, comprises the New Inn, a small post office, an old church (recently 'restored' by Victorian forebears and hosting ancient yew trees) and a handful of houses. In 1819, Michael Faraday stayed here during a tour of nearby waterfall country.

Sarn Helen is one of a number of Roman roads that criss-crossed south Wales. It starts at nearby Coelbren and marches north to the Roman fort of Y Gaer, above Brecon and on to north Wales. In a good state of preservation, it makes a fine walk in its own right across a bleak but very attractive stretch of Fforest Fawr. This stretch is the most southerly of the three sections of Sarn Helen that we follow in our walks.

Cattle drovers also used stretches of Sarn Helen in later years, especially during the 18th and 19th centuries. Cattle were taken to Brecon and then on to the Midlands for sale at auctions. Probably this use of the old route has helped keep it as an open and obvious 'way'.

For Porth yr Ogof see 'To The Gateway of the Cave'.

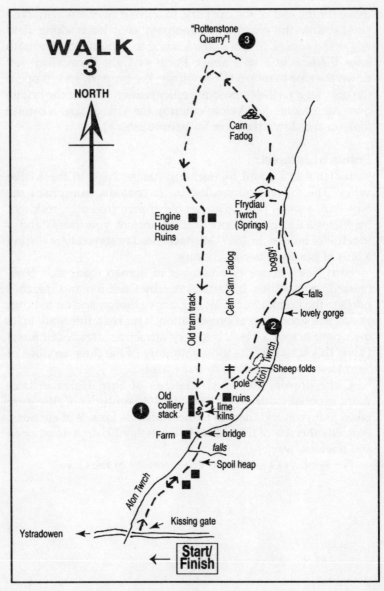

WALK
3

NORTH

"Rottenstone Quarry"! ③

Carn Fadog

Ffrydiau Twrch (Springs)

Engine House Ruins

Cefn Carn Fadog

Old tram track

boggy!

← falls

← lovely gorge

②

Afon Twrch

‡ pole

Sheep folds

Old colliery stack

■ ruins

lime kilns

①

Farm ■ ✕ ← bridge

falls

← Spoil heap

Afon Twrch

← Kissing gate

Ystradowen ←

← Start/Finish

38

To the Springs of the Wild Boar
(Ystradowen - Ffrydiau Twrch - Ystradowen)

Maps:	O S Outdoor Leisure 12 – Western Area
	Harveys Superwalker – Brecon Beacons West
Access:	The walk starts and ends near Ystradowen, between Cwmtwrch Uchaf and Cwmllynfell, on the A4068 to Brynaman.
Start/Parking:	Parking space by bridge over Afon Twrch at GR 755126
Distance/Grade:	About 7 ¹/₂ miles (12 kilometres). Moderate, but the route described crosses some remote and pathless moorland.
Terrain:	A mix, ranging from cinder tracks to pathless moor. The section leading up to the Twrch Springs is very wet, if the river is closely followed.
Facilities:	None *en route*.

The Walk:

From the car park, cross the lane to pass through a kissing gate. Follow the path along the right bank of Afon Twrch, passing some old mine buildings and the remains of an old coal tip on your right. Cross the river by a wide footbridge and turn sharp right to cross a flat pasture by the riverside. Pass through a gate into the site of the long abandoned Brynhenllys Colliery. Continue upstream to pass a row of large, derelict limekilns on your left. Pass though a kissing gate to emerge on open hillside. Take the path leading right, across the hillside, with Afon Twrch down on your right. Make for the ruins of Gelliau Farm. Climb up to position yourself behind the farm and continue, right, round the hillside to meet a path by telegraph poles. Follow the path as it contours above the river, passing below a shaly crag. Just past the crag note the stone sheepfold down below by the riverbank.

Beyond the last electricity pole (abandoned and broken) the path peters out but continue ahead across open moorland pasture for about ½ mile (800m) in the direction of a waterfall tumbling down on the right to join Afon Twrch. Start to descend to the river just before you draw level with the waterfall. Locate some flat rocks just upstream from where the waterfall tumbles into Afon Twrch. They make a natural spot for a picnic in this beautiful and rather desolate spot.

From here the going gets a bit boggy. Follow the west bank of the river upstream; it can be very wet after rain. However by ascending some twenty feet or so left, it is possible to contour the lower slopes of Cefn Carn Fadog between boulders above the wetness. Continue for a little under ½ mile (800m) to Ffrydiau Twrch up on the hillside on the left. After rain the spring presents a real drama, the water fairly tumbling out of the hillside and cascading down to the river below. To locate the spring, look for a point where a path inclines down to the river on the opposite bank, then walk up the hillside to your left (this tip becomes superfluous after rain).

From the springs continue north across open ground for about 500 yards (460 meters) and ascend west (half left) up the slopes of Carn Fadog to reach the summit shelter. There is a footpath marked on the map contouring the eastern slope of the hill but this is all but invisible on the ground. From the shelter cairn head north-west, downhill, to the abandoned quarry ahead. Just before the quarry turn left onto the old tramway leading south from the quarry entrance. Stay with the track and pass between the ruins of the old engine house, once housing the engine that hauled the trams up the incline. Continue along the track, but be aware that some sections can be very boggy underfoot; some circumnavigation through patches of rushes is called for on more than one occasion.

The track finally comes to an end just above the old limekiln and colliery ruins and spoil heaps passed earlier. Descend by the most obvious route to pass through the kissing gate. From here simply retrace your steps past the ruins, over the bridge and back to the start, alongside the banks of Afon Twrch.

Points of Interest:

Brynhenllys colliery, or what now remains of it, was opened in 1872 and closed in 1955. The prominent chimneystack was rebuilt in 1983, as a memorial to the fact that this quiet valley was once a hive of industry. *En route* to the mine ruins you will pass the spoil heaps up on your right, on the east bank of Afon Twrch. In spring there is a burst of mayflower here.

The remote Afon Twrch formed, for part of its length, the western boundary of Fforest Fawr. There is an ancient Celtic legend that King Arthur and his knights chased a wild boar (twrch is Welsh for boar) across this high tract of land, when it turned on him and gravely injured a number of his knights. The boar was an Irish prince who had earlier changed his form and had been chased across the Preseli Hills of Pembrokeshire, across Mynydd Du and on to France.

The quarry to the west of Carn Fadog was ostensibly a source of limestone from which slaked lime for agriculture was sought. However, it was also a source of 'rottenstone', perhaps better known as jewellers' rouge. This crumbly residue of limestone shales was used for polishing brass and copper and was quarried in a number of areas around the Tawe and Twrch valleys.

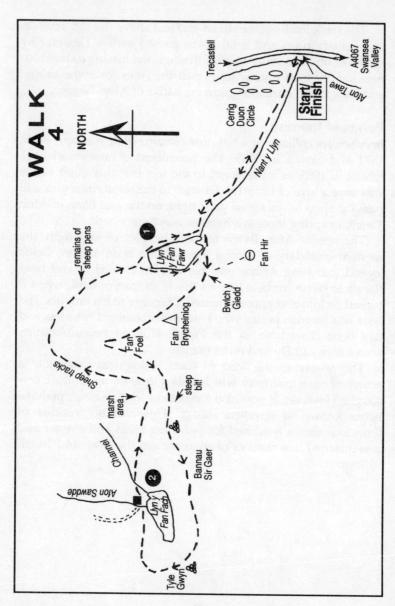

The Lady Beckons
(Trecastell Mountain Road - Llyn y Fan Fach
- Trecastell Mountain Road)

Maps:	O S Outdoor Leisure 12 – Western Area
	Harveys Superwalker – Brecon Beacons West
Access:	The walk starts and ends off the minor mountain road connecting Tafarn y Garreg to Trecastell.
Start/Parking:	Pull-in at GR 853203
Distance/Grade:	About 9 miles (14.5 kilometres). Strenuous, on account of the ascents involved (up to Fan Brycheiniog and Bannau Sir Gaer) and the length of the walk.
Terrain:	Mostly mountain paths. Indistinct in the section below Bannau Sir Gaer on the return leg but follow directions and be guided by sheep tracks.
Facilities:	None *en route*.
Note:	This area of the National Park is not actively promoted by the Park Authority due to ecological sensitivity. Please stick to the route described and redouble your efforts to follow the Country Code.

The Walk:

Leave the road, and descend a steep bank to cross the infant Afon Tawe. Scramble up the opposite bank and make for the prominent gash ahead, running down the hillside – this is Nant y Llyn, ascending steeply at first, and then gradually levelling off. As a guide, the stone circle of Cerrig Duon should be nearby on your right, and Nant y Llyn is the last gash that you come to down the hillside, when approaching from the south.

Where the ascent starts to flatten off a bit, aim half right and hold this line as you thread your way around peat bogs for about ½ mile (800 metres). High on your left is the long high ridge of Fan Hir, on your right the heights of Fan Brycheiniog. Stop at the shores of Llyn y Fan Fawr if your feet are crying out for a paddle. Behind the lake is an obvious route of ascent, up the slope ahead, leading from left to right at an angle of 45 degrees. Follow the path as it takes you up to the col of Bwlch y Giedd, nestling between Fan Hir and Fan Brycheiniog. The trampings of innumerable pairs of boots have made the ascent a little loose in places but nowhere does it present any problems if taken with care.

At the top of the col turn right and continue to the summit of Fan Brycheiniog, difficult to miss on account of a substantial stone shelter and trig point. From the summit continue northwards to the summit of Twr y Fan Foel, marked on some maps as Tro'r Fan Foel, or just Fan Foel. From here superb prospects open up in all directions. It is a splendid spot to stop for a break, to be preferred to Fan Brycheiniog for the views alone (unless inclement weather guides you to the shelter). The path now continues south-west along the scarp overlooking Cefn Bryn y Fuwch on the right, and descends fairly steeply to the gap which is the dividing line between Fan Brycheiniog to the east and Bannau Sir Gaer to the west. Cross a stream (or occasionally a dry bed), which is the very start of Afon Twrch, and ascend steeply up the slope ahead to the summit cairn of Bannau Sir Gaer. Approach the edge of the hill, from where there is a stunning view down to Llyn y Fan Fach.

Continue westwards along the top of the scarp, descending gently as you swing north to the lesser top of Tyle Gwyn. Cross Tyle Gwyn, still following the edge of the lake below, then take a grassy path heading east, downhill, and leading right to the outflow and a small stone hut. Cross the outflow and stay on the stone track to meet a man-made leat leading from the lake. Follow the leat along its left bank to cross it at a small footbridge. The path becomes a little indistinct here but by making for the foot of the scarp of Bannau Sir Gaer, ahead, and availing yourself of the number of sheep tracks you will arrive at a dry marsh below the heights (evident from a proliferation of spiky grass).

Keeping the marshy area on your left pick up a narrow path that leads between it and the base of the slope. Continue along the base of the hill and, by hopping from sheep track to sheep track, contour around the base of Twr y Fan Foel as it rises up high on your right. The path slowly becomes more obvious as it winds its way back to the northern edge of Llyn y Fan Fawr, passing, *en route*, the ruins of an ancient sheepfold.

Follow the shoreline of the lake, either east or west (the western edge under the slopes adds a little more excitement) to the outflow, then retrace your steps across the plateau, down the slope, across Afon Tawe and back to the road and the start.

Points of Interest:

Llyn y Fan Fawr is the larger of the two natural mountain lakes hereabouts and is the source of Afon Tawe. It lies at an altitude of 1,950 feet (596 metres), some 300 feet (91 metres) higher than its partner, Llyn y Fan Fach. Moraines, or piles of silt and rubble, left behind by glacial action dam both lakes. There is little aquatic vegetation or marine life in the lake, which lacks essential nutrients, although, on occasions, newts have been found here.

Llyn y Fan Fach on the other hand can knock spots off its big brother in terms of myths and legends. For it is here that lived the Lady of the Lake, one of the Tylwyth Teg (or fairy folk) of Welsh folk legend. There are, inevitably, a number of variations of this tale but in essence the story revolves around a young farm boy who, whilst tending his mother's cattle from nearby Blaen Sawdde Farm, encountered a beautiful lady, seemingly coming from the lake. After a couple of unsuccessful attempts to win her (by firstly the offering of hard oven baked bread then secondly with unbaked bread) he finally succeeded by flourishing an unleavened loaf at her. She agreed to become his bride subject to her father's approval. This would be granted on the condition that the boy could pick her out from her identical sisters. This he did, albeit with a little help from her and the marriage was agreed upon, subject to the strict proviso that if he touched her three times with iron she, and her not inconsiderable dowry, would promptly return to beneath the waters. There are no prizes for guessing the outcome, and, after the three contacts had been made, she took her toys and returned from whence she came. In the meantime, however, she bore three sons, whom she continued to see after her return to the lake, and passed to the eldest son, Rhiwallon, (named after her husband) special healing skills. It is said that Rhiwallon and his sons were the first of a line of the famous physicians of Myddfai. The line is said to have ended in 1842, with the death of Sir Rice Williams, a descendent of the family.

There is very probably a sound basis for the story. The incoming iron age Celts would almost certainly have been a cause for concern to the indigenous Neolithic locals and their iron swords and other weaponry would have been the source of many a cautionary tale. Interestingly there is an almost identical tale told, centering on the Nantlle Valley in Snowdonia. In addition, most remedies for illness would have had a herbal base and these would have been handed down from generation to generation. Bring the two themes together and you have the recipe for a good fairy tale with its basis in historical fact.

A Fan - tastic Day Out

(Blaen Llia - Fan Gyhirych - Fan Nedd - Blaen Llia)

Maps:	O S Outdoor Leisure 11 – Central Area, Brecon and the Beacons
	Harveys Superwalker – Brecon Beacons West
Access:	The walk starts and ends at Blaen Llia off the mountain road connecting Ystradfellte with Defynnog, about 2 miles (3.2 kilometres) north of Ystradfellte.
Start/Parking:	Forest Enterprise car park at GR 927165
Distance/Grade:	About 15 miles (24 kilometres). Strenuous, on account of the length involved and the challenging ascent of Fan Gyhirych.
Terrain:	Mostly good forestry and grass tracks and paths, but with some road walking. The path between Sarn Helen and Penwyllt is sometimes a little sketchy but never really in doubt. Note that there is one river crossing which, unless the river is in spate, presents no serious problems. If in spate, there is a footbridge downstream at Blaen Nedd Isaf farm, which re-connects by a waymarked path to the walk further on at the point where Sarn Helen is left.
Facilities:	None *en route.*
Note:	The walk crosses land owned by the Cnewr Estate which closes all permitted paths during the lambing season, 15th April to 10th May.

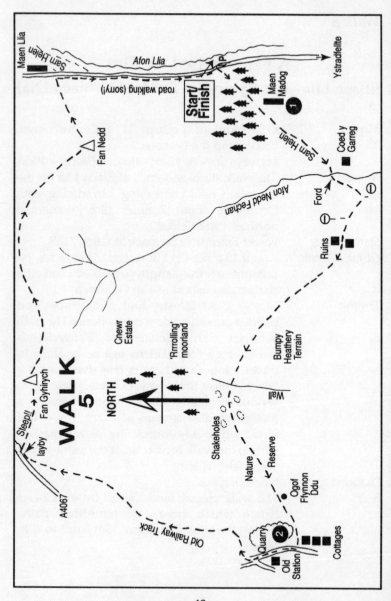

WALK 5

NORTH

Maen Llia

Sarn Helen

Afon Llia

road walking (sorry!)

P

Start/Finish

Maen Madog ①

Ystradfellte

Coed y Garreg

Sarn Helen

Ford

Ruins

Fan Nedd

Afon Nedd Fechan

Cnewr Estate

'Rrrolling' moorland

Bumpy Heathery Terrain

Wall

Fan Gyhirych

Steep!!

layby

A4067

Shakeholes

Nature Reserve

Ogof Ffynnon Ddu

Old Railway Track

Quarry ②

Old Station

Cottages

The Walk:

Leave the car park via the access track to return to the road. Turn right and, after about 300 yards (274 metres) turn left through a forest gate and on to Sarn Helen. Continue along the track through the forest (passing through the remains of a Roman camp, but you would never know it) to leave through a gate. Note the large standing stone of Maen Madog about 100 yards (92 metres) outside the forest boundary, on your left. The latin inscription referred to in 'Points of Interest' is barely traceable on the narrow south edge of the stone.

Continue unerringly along the track as, after about ³/₄ mile (1.2 kilometres) it dips down to cross the valley of Afon Nedd Fechan. Cross the river by boulder hopping, possibly slightly underwater but more negotiable to the right of the ford, and ascend the opposite hillside. Look out for, or perhaps more appropriately, listen out for, the woodpeckers around the ford. Continue along the track, to arrive at a set of gateways to an obvious junction of tracks at a forest edge (it is near this point that the footbridge path rejoins). Leave Sarn Helen at this point and turn right, crossing a stile, in the direction waymarked to Penwyllt. After about ¹/₄ mile turn left, again by a waymark post for Penwyllt, onto a less distinct grassy track. Pass between old farm ruins on your right and an abandoned railway wagon on your left and continue ahead (yet another waymark post here guides us on our way) along a path. This is a spot where buzzards are generally seen, circling and mewing overhead.

Follow the path as it crosses heather and gorse, occasionally interspersed with old field boundaries, heading north-west for about 1³/₄ miles (2.8 kilometres) after the ruins. Pass through an old gateway, then cross a wall over a stile into the Ogof Ffynnon Ddu National Nature Reserve. The path soon becomes a grassy track as it threads its way between sinkholes and grassy limestone knolls. Take care here, some of the sinkholes are very deep, manifested by the fact that a number of them have been blocked over with planks. The track crests the ridge and descends to Penwyllt and the disused quarry workings.

On arriving at the workings, and with the Penwyllt Cottages (the Headquarters of the south Wales Caving Club) on your left, turn right onto a gravel road. Follow the road, passing Penwyllt station (long disused) on your left. Pass through an open gateway onto a tarmac road, then, 10 yards/metres later, follow a footpath sign, right, onto a gravel road. Pass some sorry looking derelict cottages on your left and, where the gravel road swings sharp left, continue ahead onto grass. Keeping the quarry boundary fence on your right follow it until it guides you on to the old railway line, through a gate. Note that this is a permissive path and is closed during lambing season, as stated on the gatepost (a bit of a swine to walk this far to have to walk all the way back).

Follow the route of the old line for about $2^1/_2$ miles (4 kilometres) to the point where it meets the main A4067 road. Near the head of the valley, do not turn left down the gravel track to the main road. Instead, continue ahead to cross a stile and emerge at a lay-by at GR 868193. From the layby cross the slightly rickety stile on your right (clearly stating that this gives access to 'permitted path across Cnewr Estate'). There is also a wooden footpath marker post near the stile. From here start the grinding ascent of Fan Gyhirych by the most direct route. The climb eases (only slightly) before one last pull, to make the trig point across tussocky grass and the completion of the ascent of some 1,100 muscle wrenching feet (335 muscle wrenching metres), to a height of 2,378 feet (725 metres).

From the summit, make your way east, initially descending by a track then via a marshy col slightly to the north-west of Fan Nedd summit (at 2,175 feet – 663 metres) and ascend to the top of Fan Nedd, and a trig point. The permissive route off Fan Nedd is north-east, down boggy slopes to emerge, over a ladder stile, on the mountain road connecting Ystradfellte with Defynnog, and about 100 yards (92 metres) to the right of Maen Llia. Turn right onto the road and return to Blaen Llia and the start.

Points of Interest:

Maen Madog can frighten you half to death if you come across it in misty weather. It stands about 10 feet (3 metres) high and, in all likelihood, started its life as an 'ordinary' standing stone. Probably erected during the Bronze Age, the stone may have been a marker for the ancient trackway that later became Sarn Helen. In any event it is generally believed that the Latin inscription would have been added later, possibly during Roman times. Visible, but barely legible, the inscription translates as '(the stone) of Dervacus, son of Justus. He lies here' (You'll have to take my word for it!). Archeological excavations have failed to uncover any evidence of a human burial here.

Penwyllt is today probably best known as the home of the south Wales Caving Club. The quarry is currently disused. The long redundant railway station has a waiting room which was made specifically for Madame Adelina Patti, the Victorian diva who made her home at nearby Craig y Nos castle (see Points of Interest – Cribarth). The station itself (properly known as Craig y Nos station) was opened on 2nd September 1864, by the Neath and Brecon Railway Company. After two takeovers, one in 1877 by the Midland Railway Company, and the other in 1922 by the Great Western Railway Company, the line and station were finally closed in 1962, under the then supervision of British Railways. The station was then re-opened by Hobbs Quarries in 1964.

Just above Penwyllt is the site of the Ogof Ffynnon Ddu cave complex, one of the largest in Britain and ostensibly the reason for the National Nature Reserve, it is of considerable national and international importance.

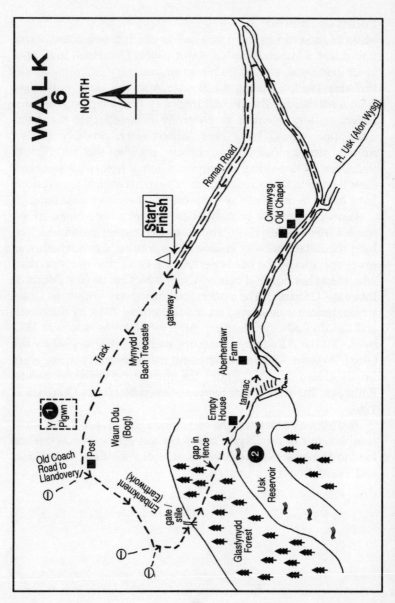

WALK 6

NORTH

R. Usk (Afon Wysg)

Roman Road

Start/Finish

Cwmwysg
Old Chapel

Track

Mynydd
Bach Trecastle

gateway

Aberhenfawr
Farm

Y Pigwn 1

Waun Ddu
(Bog!)

Empty House

tarmac

gap in fence

Old Coach
Road to
Llandovery

Post

Embankment
(Earthwork)

gate /
stile

2

Usk Reservoir

Glasfynydd
Forest

Walk 6

Where Roman Soldiers Marched
(Mynydd Bach Trecastell - Usk Reservoir
- Mynydd Bach Trecastell)

Maps:	O S Outdoor Leisure 12 – Western Area
	Harveys Superwalker – Brecon Beacons West
Access:	The walk starts and ends at Mynydd Bach Trecastell, about 1 mile (1.6 kilometres) north-east of the Usk Reservoir.
Start/Parking:	Gateway at end of tarmac lane, by a trig point. GR 846301.
Distance/Grade:	About 7 miles (11.2 kilometres). Medium
Terrain:	Moorland tracks, a little indistinct in places, forest paths and quiet lanes.
Facilities:	None *en route*.

The Walk:

Head west through the open gateway, with the trig point of Mynydd Bach Trecastell on your right. Continue ahead along a clear trackway that can be muddy in places after rain. This takes you across open moorland for about a mile (1.6 kilometres) to the site of Y Pigwn, a Roman marching camp. The camp can be identified by a series of grassy hummocks fringing the hillside to your right. Continue ahead past the camp for about 50 yards (46 metres).

Fork half left, at a Brecon Beacons National Park waymark post, on to a less distinct grassy track (the track ahead and to the right is an old coach road joining Trecastell to Llandymddyfri and pre-dating the present route of the A40 – oxen were used to pull the coaches up the incline). Continue along this track as it contours to the left of a hill (un-named on the 1:25000 map).

Keeping the bog of Waun Ddu well to your left, pass a series of ancient earthworks and a prominent ditch, also on your left. Where the earthworks end continue ahead, crossing the head of a small stream to meet a track at right angles. Turn left onto the track and follow it gently downhill to the northern boundary of the Glasfynydd Forest. Cross over a stile to the right of a green metal gate and continue ahead. Follow the track ahead and downhill, ignoring tempting little paths leading off into the forest (so nearly perished Hansel and Gretel). After about 1/2 mile (800 metres) look out for, and follow, signs indicating a temporary bridleway. Pass through a clear gap in the fence ahead onto a tarmac forestry road. Turn left to follow the northern edge of the Usk Reservoir for about 3/4 mile (1.2 kilometres) to the dam. With the dam on your right follow the road down to the bridge crossing the reservoir outflow. This is the River Usk (Afon Wysg), its majesty at this point somewhat humbled by man's intervention in his quest for water supplies.

Don't cross the bridge but continue instead along the country lane ahead. Stay with the lane as it twists and turns along the valley for about 2 1/2 miles (4 kilometres) keeping the river down on your right. The lane passes through the hamlet of Cwmwysg. Don't be tempted to try a short cut back to the start by one of the tracks or footpaths shown on the OS map as leading off to the left. They are all fenced off in their upper reaches and, in any case, the routes across the fields are not at all clear. Stay with the lane for a further mile past Cwmwysg, then turn left up a narrow lane, which joins up with the Roman road encountered earlier when heading for the start of the walk. Turn left onto the road and follow it back to the trig point and the start of the walk.

Points of Interest:

It is difficult to conjure up an image of a Roman marching camp in this isolated and somewhat desolate spot, accommodating up to maybe 10,000 tents. Yet, in its day, Y Pigwn was an important strategic site for the Roman army trying to maintain its grip over the still warring Silures. Rather than being permanently garrisoned, the camp would only really be fully occupied when used as a staging post for the legionaries when on the move. It is, however, still a site of significant historical interest, and catches the walker quite unawares.

Usk Reservoir, inaugurated in 1955 by Queen Elizabeth II, has a capacity of up to 2,700 million gallons. It was built to supply water to the city of Swansea, along with the Crai Reservoir some six miles to the south-east, as the crow flies. Both rainbow and brown trout attract fishermen to the reservoir, which is also a spawning ground for salmon. Walkers can also enjoy the shoreline path and waymarked trails in the surrounding Glasfynydd Forest.

WALK 7

NORTH

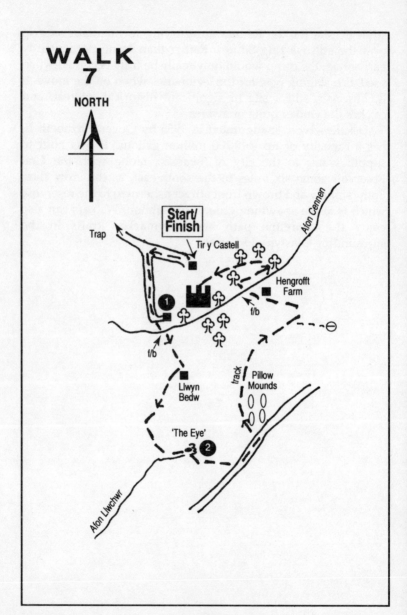

Trap

Start/Finish

Tir y Castell

Afon Cennen

Hengrofft Farm

f/b

1

f/b

Llwyn Bedw

track

Pillow Mounds

'The Eye'

2

Afon Llwchwr

Walk 7

Around Loughor's Eye
(A Circuit around Carreg Cennen Castle)

Maps:	O S Outdoor Leisure 12 – Western Area
	Harveys Superwalker – Brecon Beacons West
Access:	The walk starts and ends at the car park below the imposing structure of Carreg Cennen Castle, near the village of Trap.
Start/Parking:	Carreg Cennen Castle car park GR 667194
Distance/Grade:	About 4¹/₂ miles (7 kilometres). Easy.
Terrain:	Mostly grass tracks and paths, but with some stretches of path indistinct on the ground.
Facilities:	Tir y Castell farm has a small but very pleasant tea-room and souvenir shop, along with a friendly dog, a peacock, and a very tame one-legged jackdaw that will eat from your hand, sit on your head etc. The farm also hosts a small number of rare breeds, including some incredible longhorn cattle. There are loos at the car park.
	The Cennen Arms in nearby Trap also serves a very good lunch and is worth a visit.
Note:	This is a gem of a walk if timed for either a fine spring or autumn day. Also note that admission charges to the castle are payable at Tir y Castell Farm, who administer on behalf of Cadw, the Welsh Ancient Monuments body.

The Walk:
Leave the car park by the way you came in, and turn left along the lane. At the next junction turn left, downhill, towards Afon

Cennen at the bottom of the valley. After about ¹/₂ mile (800 metres) cross a stile in the hedge almost immediately before Pant-y-Fynnon Cottage. Go straight down across the fields to the river, crossing two more stiles *en route*. Cross Afon Cennen over a footbridge, and continue ahead, through a gate, to the farm of Llwyn-bedw. Turn right onto the farm track, following it through fields to ford a stream. Continue uphill to meet a junction. Take the left turn through a gate, and follow the track as far as a stream and stone bridge. Continue ahead and uphill, to pick up a stream. Follow its course to reach the source of Afon Llwchwr. There is a cave here known as Llygad Llwchwr (Eye of Loughor). I am told that it is navigable but only by experienced cavers – admire, and move on!

Continue along the track, passing a disused limekiln. Just past the kiln the track comes to an end. Follow the line of a stone wall passing between two sink holes. Continue ahead to a drystone wall running along a mountain road. Follow the wall, left, to a stile. Cross the stile and turn left into the road.

Follow the road for about 100 yards (92 metres) and turn left onto a grass track past some ancient pillow mounds (I always believed these were for farming rabbits, but the map marks them as 'Beddau'r Derwyddon', or druid graves, so keep looking over your shoulder!). Continue along the track to cross a stile, a stream and a second stile on your right into a field. Cross the length of the field to a gate on the far side and a National Park sign. Follow the waymarked path as you descend to Hen-grofft Farm. Pass through the farmyard then on to a minor road to cross a bridge over Afon Cennen. Turn immediately right onto a path and follow the river upstream to join a waymarked path on the left. Climb back on yourself, through woodland, to emerge at a gate just below the castle at the cliff top. Either turn left and up to the castle or right, down the path leading back to Tir y Castell farm and the start.

Points of Interest:

The castle at Carreg Cennen (in the care of Cadw) is a superbly imposing structure, built on a limestone hill with a 300 foot (92 metre) cliff dropping sheer away on the southern side. Access to the castle is by ticket, purchased at Tir y Castell Farm, near the car park. The castle was originally built in 1197. In 1248 Rhys Fychan captured the castle from its Norman holders but in 1277 they regained it. It was almost entirely rebuilt in 1284 by the Giffard family when they were presented with the castle by Edward 1st. The reconstruction included an outer wall, the base of which can just be made out to the left of the entrance bridgeway. However, as was the way of things in those days, the Giffards fell out of favour and the castle came into the Despenser family. In 1403 the ubiquitous Owain Glyndŵr attacked the castle, damaging it somewhat during the proceedings. In 1462, however, the Yorkists employed 500 men, at a recorded cost of £28, to finish off what Glyndŵr had started and rendered the castle completely unusable by local bandits (or anyone else who fancied grabbing it). This was borne slightly out of sour grapes as the Lancastrians had holed up here during the Wars of the Roses.

Make a point of visiting the cave in the south-eastern corner of the castle. Access is via a tunnel cut into the cliff face. The use of the cave is unclear; it may have been some form of columbarium for keeping pigeons or possibly even a dungeon. In any event it predates the castle, the bones of four Stone Age skeletons being found there.

Deeper into the hillside there are reputed to be caves occupied by the sleeping Owain Lawgoch (Owain of the Red Hand), who will wake and come to Wales' aid when she needs him. This is a very similar legend to the tale of the sleeping King Arthur and his knights under Dinas Rock, just outside Pontneddfechan, in the Neath Valley (and many other places).

Llygad Llwchwr (Eye of Loughor) is the source of Afon Llwchwr, which flows down to the sea at Casllwchwr (Loughor) in Carmarthen Bay. There is a story that an underground river connects Llyn y Fan Fach, under the heights of Bannau Sir Gaer, to the 'Eye'. It was once certainly possible (and, I am told, still is) for experienced cavers to explore the river underground as far as a series of chambers under the hillside, but how far it is possible to venture I don't know, and have no appetite to find out!

Clambering over Cribarth
(Craig y Nos – Cribarth – Craig y Nos)

Maps:	O S Outdoor Leisure 11 – Central Area, Brecon and the Beacons
	Harveys Superwalker – Brecon Beacons West
Access:	The walk starts and ends at Craig y Nos, in the upper reaches of Dyffryn Tawe (the Swansea Valley) on the A4067
Start/Parking:	Either the National Park car park (Pay and Display) or a layby next to Craig y Nos Castle at GR 841153 (room for about 8 cars).
Distance/Grade:	About 4 miles (6.4 kilometres). Easy, with the one exception of the ascent of Cribarth, and that is not too bad.
Terrain:	Good footpaths, well waymarked. Path a little vague on Cribarth ridge and on part of the return leg, but no serious navigational problems. The last few hundred yards return along a main road but present no danger if walked on the verges (unfortunately there is no right of way through the adjacent fields).
Facilities:	None *en route*, but Dan yr Ogof showcaves are nearby (closed in the winter season), and the Gwyn Arms and Tafarn y Garreg are about a mile up the road from Craig y Nos.
Note:	This is a fine walk for a crisp autumn day, when the bracken has turned from its summer green to a deep russet colour. Short, sharp and entirely satisfying!

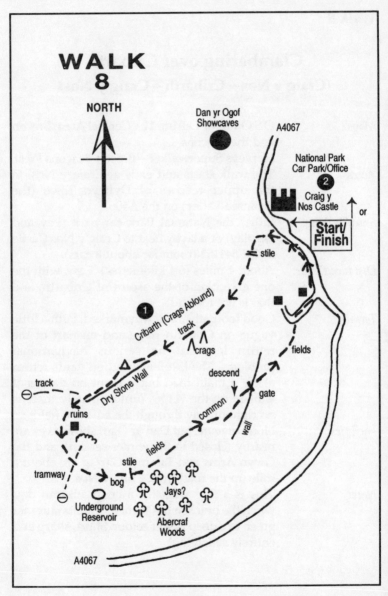

WALK
8

NORTH

Dan yr Ogof
Showcaves

A4067

National Park
Car Park/Office

2

Craig y
Nos Castle

or

Start/
Finish

stile

Cribarth (Crags Ablound)

1

track

crags

fields

descend

gate

track

Dry Stone Wall

ruins

common

wall

fields

tramway

stile

bog

Jays?

Underground
Reservoir

Abercraf
Woods

A4067

The Walk:

Leave the layby from the entrance furthest from Craig y Nos Castle, cross the main road and turn left. After about 10 yards/metres turn right through a gap in the wall and cross a double stile. Turn left up a track and, 50 yards (46 metres) later turn sharp right up a path waymarked 'To Open Hill'. The path is clearly marked with white painted posts.

Follow the path as it winds its way up the north-eastern slope of Cribarth, offering superb views of both Craig y Nos Castle and the very top of Dyffryn Tawe, dominated by Fan Gyhirych. Near the top of the climb the path splits, just before a solitary hawthorn tree. Follow the path that continues to ascend alongside the fence, and cross a stile in a dry stone wall. The stile has a plaque bearing the words, 'New route for guide book walks' – very helpful! Once over the stile, bear half right and continue to ascend over open ground to the crest of the ridge of Cribarth. The hill may be relatively low at 1,388 feet (423 metres) but its summit is surely one of the busiest and most interesting in the Park, pock marked, as it is, with old quarry workings. From the top, turn right along the ridge to the highest spot, marked by a trig point (OSBM S2024) and a prominent shelter cairn. Pick your own route to the trig point, but there is a tram track that almost leads you there. Take care in mist; the quarry workings can loom up on you quite unexpectedly.

From the trig point the safest line of descent is to continue ahead (south-west) for a short distance and make your way to the left down a grass slope to the well maintained dry stone wall below. Follow the line of the wall to where the slope levels off and the wall turns sharp left. Continue ahead along a raised tram track for about 10 yards/metres and then turn left along a faint path, keeping the wall and fence about 20 yards (18 metres) away on your left. After about 50 yards (46 metres) the path descends to a stile in the fence, marked by a wooden waymark post. Cross the stile and turn right to follow a grass path, which contours the southern slopes of Cribarth. Look out for what appear to be the remains of an old farmstead here.

Where the path meets a tramway coming down the hillside, (the spot readily identified by a rather stumpy waymark post, at knee level) turn right and descend along the tramway for about 10 yards/metres, then turn left, and continue on around the hillside. Do not cross over the stile (waymarked to Abercrave) at the point where the tramway meets a fence. The correct path is signposted to Ynyswen. Follow the path as it gently descends, over rather slabby rock in places, to meet a stile leading into a field on the left (passing, first, an underground reservoir on the right). The approach to the stile can be very boggy!

Cross the stile into the field, keeping a stone wall and woodland on your right. Look (and listen) out for jays (known in Welsh as Sgrech y Coed, the screecher of the wood) here. Cross the field to leave over a second stile and continue ahead across the next field, still keeping the wall on your right. Cross over a third stile, continue across the field, and leave by a fourth stile, this time back into open moorland.

Continue ahead along a vague path, keeping a fence on your left. Where the fence turns sharp left up the hillside, cross a broken stone wall (look for a waymark arrow on the corner fencepost), climb gently for about 20 yards (18 metres) then follow the path to the right as it continues to contour the eastern flanks of Cribarth. Cross a stile in a stone wall, and continue ahead on an even vaguer path. About 500 yards (450 metres) past the stile, trend right to pick up a more obvious path descending to a stone wall below on your right. As a guide, the short descent to the wall starts opposite an obvious grassy slope descending from Cribarth's summit ridge, flanked by two prominent limestone crags. Pass through an iron gate in the wall and continue to descend, through bracken. About 100 yards (92 metres) after the gate, the path swings sharp right, over the remains of a stone wall. About 50 yards (46 metres) later swing sharp left and continue the descent down a more obvious track.

At the next junction of paths, clearly marked with waymark

posts, take the left turn, marked as a bridleway, and confirmed by a waymark arrow nailed to the fourth tree on your right. Follow the path over a tumbledown stone wall and continue ahead to cross an iron stile. Continue ahead in the direction of the waymark arrow. Turn $1/2$ left to pick up a vague track across a field and exit over a stile beside a gate. The track becomes more pronounced and exits the field over a stile and into a tarmac lane.

Turn right and follow the lane down to the main A4067 road. From here turn left and, keeping to the grass verge, return to the start of the walk at Craig y Nos.

Points of Interest:

Cribarth is well worth the climb if only for the superb views up the Upper Swansea (or Tawe) valley, and down to Craig y Nos Castle. Whilst of modest height (only 1,388 feet/423 metres) it is a ridge that amply repays exploration. It provides an interesting spot for a picnic, excellent facilities for hide and seek and a busy study site for industrial archaeologists. The rock is limestone and was clearly the subject of extensive quarrying around the turn of the last century. A major fault in the limestone runs north-east from here. Whilst of no particular consequence, you may wish to know that I picked up the only fossil (of a sea shell) that I have ever found in the Park on Cribarth's craggy top.

The main part of Craig y Nos (the 'Rock of the Night') Castle was built in 1842, but is far better known as the home of the Spanish opera diva, Adela Juana Maria Patti. She bought the castle in 1878 from a Mr. Morgan Morgan, and remained its owner until her death there on 27th September 1919, at the age of 76. In 1891 Madame Adelina Patti (as she was now known) built her own theatre at the castle, soon joined by a large conservatory. This was subsequently donated by her to the town of Swansea, where it is now known as the Patti Pavilion. She was buried at Pere Lachaise cemetery in Paris but throughout her life came to love Craig y Nos as her 'real' home.

After her death, the castle was used as a hospital but, in 1976, the grounds were opened to the public, under the management of the National Park Authority (or, in those days, Committee).

To The Gateway of the Cave
(Gwaun Hepste - Sgwd Clungwyn
- Porth yr Ogof - Gwaun Hepste)

A short and pleasant walk, perhaps best left for when the weather really isn't trying as hard as it might

Maps:	OS Outdoor Leisure 11 – Brecon Beacons, Central Area
	Harveys Superwalker – Brecon Beacons West
Access:	The walk starts and ends at the Forest Enterprise car park at Gwaun Hepste off the minor road from Penderyn to Ystradfellte
Start/Parking:	Car Park at GR 935125
Distance/Grade:	About 3½ miles (5.6 kilometres). Easy. A pleasant stroll through a wood and alongside a river, to return by way of a country lane
Terrain:	Mostly good tracks and paths, but with some road walking. Expect mud after periods of rain, especially on the return leg from Porth yr Ogof, rendering some stretches slippery. Take care and no problems should arise.
Facilities:	Loos at the Porth yr Ogof car park. Information Board also at the start with useful information on the area.
Note:	Both the car parks at Gwaun Hepste and Porth yr Ogof are managed by the National Park Authority and there is a charge (£3 for any length of time at the time of writing). This may appear steep but because the sites are manned this significantly minimises the risk of vehicle break in. (Note however that

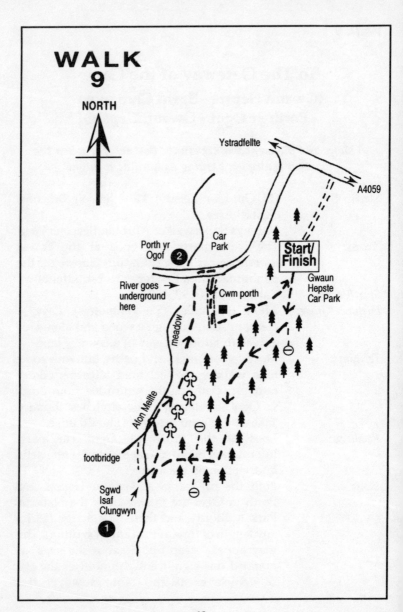

WALK
9

NORTH

Ystradfellte

A4059

Car Park

Porth yr Ogof ②

Start/Finish

River goes underground here

Cwm porth

Gwaun Hepste Car Park

meadow

Afon Mellte

footbridge

Sgwd Isaf Clungwyn ①

Gwaun Hepste car park is not manned from October to April).

The Walk:

Leave the car park in the opposite direction to the entrance and pass to the right of the information boards, picking up the red waymark arrow on the post nearby. Pass through a second car park and barbecue site, then follow the narrow path through trees for several hundred yards to meet a broad gravel forest track. Turn right onto the track and continue ahead ignoring a junction of paths (signposted right to Porth yr Ogof and left to Bryn Cul). Stay with the track until you meet a path leading off right indicated by a red arrow on a waymark post. Follow the path as it leads downhill through the forest and then swings left to contour the hillside. The path then swings right, again downhill, to meet a junction of paths. Cross the junction and follow the descending path ahead, keeping a narrow stream on your left. At the next junction continue ahead, between wooden fences, down to a viewing point overlooking the Sgwd Uchaf Clungwyn falls (sometimes just referred to as Sgwd Clungwyn).

From here retrace your steps and, back at the junction, turn left to follow Afon Mellte upstream. The path at this point is fairly high above the river but slowly descends to meet it just before a wooden footbridge on your left. Do not cross the footbridge but follow the path ahead as it weaves its way in between the river on the left and a fenced off marsh meadow on the right. Pass through a gate and enter woodland, the river still close on your left. The path leaves the woodland and again becomes squeezed between the river and a fenced off meadow on the right. Follow it right to the point where it meets the tarmac lane by the car park at Porth yr Ogof.

To explore the cavernous mouth of the cave, cross the lane to the car park, and follow a waymarked path to the left of the car park. At the far end of the car park are information boards telling you all about the cave and warning (in dire tones) of the potential dangers hereabouts. From the boards, steeply descend the obvious path (either over the stiles or through the gate) and turn left at the bottom. The cave entrance is now in front of you.

From the cave return to the car park by the way you came and walk back to the entrance. Turn left up the lane and twenty yards later turn right onto a farm track, waymarked to Gwaun Hepste. Cross over a stile and pass Cwmporth Farm on your right. Continue ahead along the track for about fifty yards and turn left, over a stile, onto a path waymarked to Gwaun Hepste. Climb gently uphill keeping a fence on your left and forestry on your right. Where the path levels out at a junction turn left, indicated by a red waymark arrow (the mud is really juicy here). Follow the path, keeping a fence on your left. At the next waymark post turn right and continue along the path. Turn left at the next waymark post, then right at the next post, this time the red arrow being joined by a brown arrow (the arrows indicate waymarked trails through the forest). Stay with the path as it delivers you safely back to the car park and the start.

Points of Interest:
The falls of Sgwd Uchaf Clungwyn are on Afon Mellte, a name it certainly lives up to as it thunders and crashes its way down to join Afon Nedd. The word 'uchaf' means upper and distinguishes the falls from the 'isaf' or Lower Clungwyn Falls. The falls drop for some 30 feet (9 metres) over a fault in the hard sandstone and millstone grit, giving the river access to soft shales which can be clearly seen from the western bank (accessible by crossing the footbridge upstream and following the path back down on the opposite bank). The falls have two stages or 'steps', the second falling quite a bit further than the first.

Porth yr Ogof (Gateway of the Cave) looks for all the world like a huge, hungry, gaping mouth constantly swallowing up all that Afon Mellte can throw at it. Also known by some as White Horse cave, on account of some calcite streaks shaped like a horse's head within the main chamber, the cave is quite considerable, extending back over 200 feet (61 metres), and is reckoned to be the largest cave entrance in Wales, measuring some 50 feet (15 metres) wide by 16 feet (5 metres) high. It is quite possible to explore the entrance chamber but a number of passages lead off, which should not be tackled unless you are in a competently led caving party. The various notices that grimly warn of fatalities really are not bluffing; people have come horribly unstuck (or stuck here, depending upon ones' perspective) when venturing outside the bounds of their competence. Do read the information boards and be aware of the dangers. All that said, there is a feeling of awe engendered by the size of this natural gaping mouth – just sit on the flat limestone and take it all in.

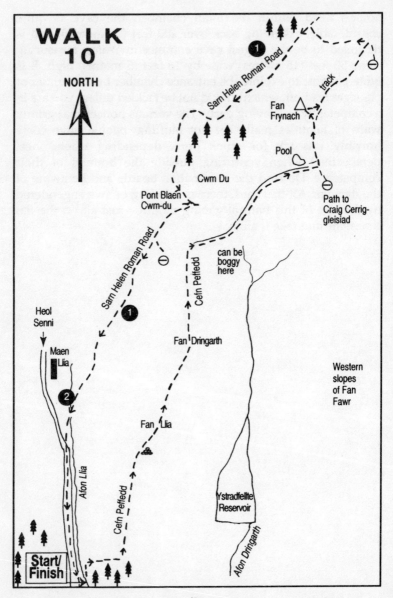

WALK 10

NORTH

Sarn Helen Roman Road

Fan Frynach

Pool

Cwm Du

Path to Craig Cerrig-gleisiad

Pont Blaen Cwm-du

can be boggy here

Cefn Perfedd

Fan Dringarth

Heol Senni

Maen Llia

Sarn Helen Roman Road

Fan Llia

Western slopes of Fan Fawr

Afon Llia

Cefn Perfedd

Ystradfellte Reservoir

Afon Dringarth

Start/Finish

Over the Fans and Back on the Track
(Blaen Llia - Fan Llia - Fan Frynach - Blaen Llia)

Maps:	O S Outdoor Leisure 11 – Central Area, Brecon and the Beacons
	Harveys Superwalker – Brecon Beacons West
Access:	The walk starts and ends at Blaen Llia off the mountain road connecting Ystradfellte with Defynnog, about 2 miles (3.2 kilometres) north of Ystradfellte.
Start/Parking:	Forest Enterprise car park at GR 927165
Distance/Grade:	About 11 miles (17.7 kilometres). Strenuous, more on account of the length of the walk than the ascents involved, which are fairly mild. The longest ascent is to Fan Llia summit from the start, a climb of some 900 feet (274 metres).
Terrain:	Mostly clear mountain paths and obvious tracks. Path a little vague up Fan Llia but general direction is obvious (i.e. up!). The return leg involves about $1^1/_2$ miles (2.4 kilometres) of tarmac trotting along a quiet road.
Facilities:	None *en route*.

The Walk:

From the car park cross Afon Llia by way of a ford (there used to be a bridge here!). Turn immediately left and cross a stile. About 5 yards/metres later cross a second stile, right, into a scrubby plantation. Follow the path as it ascends half left through the plantation, to leave it over a third stile. The advised path turns right here and directly ascends to the ridge of Cefn Perfedd, keeping the fence and forestry on the right. The path is not obvious but, as an old pop song has it, the only way is up.

On cresting the ridge turn left and follow it through rough grass to slowly and gradually ascend to the prominent cairn marking the southern end of the summit of Fan Llia (Llia was the sister of King Brychan). As a guide, trend to the left of the ridge, on the Afon Llia side, to more easily gain the track that takes you to the top. From the cairn continue ahead in a north-easterly direction along a more obvious grass track, passing over Fan Llia's highest point (2,073 feet – 632 metres) and crossing (although you would hardly realise it) the top of Fan Tringarth.

The route now lies along the grass track that runs north following the ridge, again named on the map as Cefn Perfedd. Keep ahead on the track, ignoring one or two tracks leading off to the left. At the northern head of the ridge the track ends at a path running from left to right. Turn right and gently descend to the saddle separating Nant Cwm Du from Afon Tringarth. Ascend the path (a bit scruffy here) on the far side and, after about 100 yards (92 metres), turn left onto a sheeptrack to aim for a fence. Keeping the fence on your left continue ahead. The fence is there, I guess, to prevent sheep (or you) from tumbling in a very undignified manner over the cliffs of Craig Cwm- du.

From here the fence is your guide as you follow the path for about a mile to a junction of paths just north of Craig Cerrig-gleisiad. Pass through the gate on your left and gently ascend a rough stony track (to your left here is a rather pleasant pond – busy with dragon flies in the summer, and a rather pleasing picnic spot anyway). Follow the track as it gently winds its way uphill and, after about 200 yards, (180 metres) take a footpath leading off to the left. Follow the path as it leads you unerringly to the summit trig point of Fan Frynach (OSBM S2511). A bronze plaque on the east face of the trig point informs you that it was adopted by the 1075 Camberley Squadron Air Cadets in July 1994.

From the trig point return to the track by following the path leading east – Pen y Fan and Corn Du in your sights. On rejoining the track turn left and follow it as it descends north-easterly to eventually swing round to the west at a junction of two gates and a stile. Continue downhill, staying with the track, to be delivered safely to the old Roman road of Sarn Helen, meeting it at right angles.

Turn left onto Sarn Helen. This is now the route back to the start as it contours the western flanks of Bannau Frynach, Tringarth and Llia. One word of warning, however. Following the uphill climb after crossing Pont Cwm Du do not take a fork off to the left, uphill. Instead, continue along the more obvious route ahead. That navigational challenge behind you, just continue to follow Sarn Helen as it takes you gently back and deposits you onto the Ystradfellte to Defynnog mountain road.

At the road turn left and after about $1^1/_2$ miles (2.4 kilometres) find yourself back at the start.

Points of Interest:

Sarn Helen is one of a number of Roman roads that criss-crossed Wales. It starts at nearby Coelbren and marches north to the Roman fort of Y Gaer, above Brecon, and on to the north. In a good state of preservation, it makes a fine walk in its own right across a bleak but very attractive stretch of Fforest Fawr. Stretches of the 'Sarn', or 'way' were also adopted as drove roads during the 18th and 19th centuries.

Maen Llia, near the point where Sarn Helen joins the road, is a solitary standing stone erected, it is believed, during the Bronze Age. The stone measures around twelve feet high by nine feet wide (3.6 metres by 2.7 metres) and, if you believe a good story, ambles over to the nearby river for a drink when it hears the cock crow. Luckily, there are not too many cocks crowing hereabouts.

Bibliography

Brecon Beacons National Park Scenery – A Geological Interpretation by D Emlyn Evans. Published by the National Museum of Wales in conjunction with the Brecon Beacons National Park Joint Advisory Committee

Exploring the Brecon Beacons, Black Mountains and Waterfall Country by Chris Barber. Published by Regional Publications (Bristol) Ltd.

The Romance of the Welsh Mountains by Chris Barber. Published by Blorenge Books

Portrait of the Brecon Beacons by Edmund J Mason. Published by Robert Hale

The Brecon Beacons National Park by Roger Thomas. Published by Webb and Bower

Brecon Beacons National Park (National Park Guide No. 5) edited by Margaret Davies. Published by Her Majesty's Stationery Office

The Story of Brecknock by Wendy Hughes. Published by Gwasg Carreg Gwalch

The Mountains of England and Wales. Volume 1 – Wales by John and Anne Nuttall. Published by Cicerone Press